To: ______________________________

From: ______________________________

Start Date: ______________________________

Accountability Partner:

____

Draw Closer to God

31-Day Journal Challenge for Women

Crystal S. Daye

ISBN: 978-1-953759-31-3 (paperback)

Cover Design and Interior Book Layout by: HCP Book Publishing

Table of Contents

Acknowledgement

First and foremost, I want to give GOD thanks for blessing me with the favor and grace to walk boldly in my purpose and be able to impact others through my writing. It is truly an honor to know He orders my steps, and all things are working together for my good.

Secondly, to everyone who will read this book, I truly appreciate you!

Introduction

As a believer, we have an awesome privilege to develop an intimate relationship with God (our good Father). It might seem like a small thing to some but when you know the Creator of the universe who knew us before we were formed in our mother's womb (See Jeremiah 1:5, Psalm 139:13) and who knows how sinful we are because we fail Him every day (See Romans 3:23), yet He loves us so much by sending His Son to save us from eternal separation and damnation (See John 3:16), we should truly spend our lives serving Him, praising Him and being grateful that He still desires that we have a relationship with Him.

> *Draw near to God, and he will draw near to you. Cleanse your hands, you sinners, and purify your hearts, you double-minded. (James 4:8 – ESV).*

The above Scripture highlights that it is up to us to maintain this relationship and intimacy. God never moves; He is always waiting for us to come closer to Him. When we desire to draw closer to God, we desire to commune, fellowship, and reconcile with God. Christ's death, burial, and resurrection was to do exactly that; reconcile God and man through Christ.

Over the next thirty-one days, we will look at the ways we can develop intimacy with God through prayer, praise, the Word, etc. The purpose of this devotional is for you to cultivate a daily habit of spending time with God while strengthening your faith.

There is never a day we do not need GOD. Daily we need His direction, wisdom, clarity, breakthrough, guidance, provisions, grace, mercy and forgiveness. God desires a relationship with us. From the beginning with Adam and Eve, that has always been His desire but, after the fall, we were separated and as a result, we continuously desire other things more than God. Therefore, we must become INTENTIONAL because distractions coupled with the innate lack of desire for godliness can make it hard for us to develop intimacy with God. So, yes, I urge you to start praying for a deeper desire for God.

Again, I encourage you to remain committed to the end of this challenge. You should find a partner and hold each other accountable to ensure you complete it. Let this be the beginning of a new level in your journey with Jesus Christ.

I love you and God loves you more!

Crystal Daye

DAY 1
Let God Interrupt Your Routine

Ask me and I will tell you remarkable secrets you do not know about things to come. **Jeremiah 33:3**

This 31-Day Journal Challenge will require sacrifice for many. Most of us already have busy days and trying to cram twenty minutes into our schedule will seem impossible. But, my friend, we must be the kind of women who make spending time with God the most important part of our routine.

Everyone struggles with quiet-time consistency from time to time. Know that if you are struggling with it, you are not alone!

I know how being interrupted can be impolite but when God interrupts, it is the best thing that could happen for us. God has a much bigger plan than we can imagine; so, it is important that we ask God to take control, lead and direct us daily. If we want to draw closer to God, we must get out of our comfort zone and allow Him to take over our daily routine.

Prayer

Dear Lord, I commit the next 31 days to You. I commit to completing this challenge because I really want to draw closer to You. As I commence this challenge, I ask that You interrupt my routine as You see fit. I know Lord that Your plans for me are greater, so I humble myself now and allow You to lead. Have Your way in my life. In Jesus' name. Amen.

Journal Challenge

a. How do you plan on making extra time for God over the next four weeks?
b. What are some of the plans you believe God has placed on your heart about your life?
c. Write a prayer asking God to show you how to draw closer to Him.

Reflection Song for the Day: Press In Your Presence by Shana Wilson.

Journal With God

DAY 2
Seek The Lord

Seek the Lord while you can find him. Call on him now while he is near. ***Isaiah 55:6***

How can an omnipresent God get lost for us to "seek" Him? This verse sounds like it is for unbelievers who do not know God. These are thoughts to ponder.

When we look at our daily lives and everything going on around the world, we will hear many ask, "Where is God?" We know God is always with us but many times our unconfessed sins, distractions and busyness can block us from experiencing His presence.

Seeking God is about seeking His presence. This is a personal experience through pleading and calling on Him to reveal His glory to us, for us to experience His daily revelations and directions.

Prayer

Father God, I can get so preoccupied with my own urgencies and with seeking solutions and remedies from

Your hand. My daily needs can sometimes overwhelm me. Help me to change my focus. Help me to seek Your face and to look to You for strength to walk where I need to walk. Help me to seek to know You better. Thank You for Your loving patience with me. I ask this in Jesus' name. Amen.

Journal Challenge

a. Reflect on the last time you truly experienced God on another level. Describe that experience. How did you feel? What was it like?
b. Why do you think you don't have that experience more often?
c. How can you implement today's verse into how you can begin to allow God to interrupt your daily routine?

Reflection Song of the Day: The More I Seek You by Kari Jobe.

Journal With God

Day 3
Embracing God's Love

For this is how God loved the world: He gave his one and only Son, so that everyone who believes in him will not perish but have eternal life. ***John 3:16***

Do you realize how much God loves you? It is easy to believe that God loves others, but do you truly understand His love for you? We get so caught up with our past that we think our past hinders us from receiving God's grace. Not true. God said His grace is sufficient. "Sufficient" means more than enough. Nothing you have done is too much for God to forgive. This mindset holds us captive and disrupts our walk with God. Understand, accept and embrace that the Creator of the Universe thinks you are to die for (literally).

God created YOU because He loves you. The good news is that God loves you on your good days as much as He loves you on your bad days. He loves you when you can feel His love, and He loves you when you can't seem to feel His love. He loves you regardless of whether or not you think you deserve His love.

Prayer

Dear heavenly Father, for most of my life I have tried to earn Your love and gain Your approval. Father, forgive me for misrepresenting Your Father-heart of love and thank You for showing me that Your love for me is not dependent on what I can do for You, but rests entirely on what the Lord Jesus did for me on the cross. Thank You for Your unconditional love, in Jesus' name. Amen.

Journal Challenge

a. What are some of the thoughts that plague you to doubt God's love?
b. Now, take a red ink pen and cross out ALL those lies and write seven times - GOD LOVES ME.
c. Mediate and journal what John 3:16 means to you.

Reflection Song of the day: How He loves Us by Jesus Culture and Kim Walker.

God's unconditional love is a very difficult concept for people to accept because there is always payment for everything we receive in the world. It is just how things work here. But GOD is not like people! Embrace His love!

Journal With God

Day 4
What Is Holding You Back?

This means that anyone who belongs to Christ has become a new person. The old life is gone; a new life has begun. ***2 Corinthians 5:17***

I have always admired Christians while I was growing up. I knew there was a God because I prayed a lot and have seen Him come through for me many times, but I was too fearful to even consider taking the step to surrender my life to the Lord. Honestly, I thought I needed to clean up my life; stop partying, stop fornicating, stop lying, etc. I also held on to so many things (friends, clothes) that I felt I was not ready to let go. But one Friday afternoon, the Pastor of a church I was visiting called me and asked me a simple but profound question that changed my life forever: "What if you die tomorrow, what would be the excuse you would give to the Lord for not accepting His gift of salvation?"

Suddenly, going to hell for a boyfriend, friends, partying, drinking and sex just never seemed worth it.

Many times, we think we need to get right before we can draw close to God, but the Bible says Jesus died to save the unrighteous and His death gives us the opportunity to have a relationship with Him. If we could clean up ourselves then what would be the reason for Jesus dying for our sins?

Once we accept Jesus as our Lord and Savior, He will make us new. Only Jesus is the way to the Father and only He can change our address from the snares and torment of Hell to a glorious life in Heaven. So, the question is, "What is holding you back?"

If you are already baptized and still living part-time for Christ, remember that in Christ you can either be hot or cold but never lukewarm. Start praying that the Holy Spirit will reside in you and you will be convicted to let go of whatever is holding you back.

Today's Prayer

Father, I pray against every fear and doubt that is crippling me from surrendering my life completely to You. Lord, nothing that is holding me back is worth more than You, so help me today to let it ALL go. In Jesus' name. Amen.

Journal Challenge

a. Today, write down ALL the things that are holding you back from totally surrendering your life to God.

b. Write out the verse Romans 6:23 and meditate on it.
c. Pray and ask the Lord to give you the courage to make the step to accept His true gift of salvation today and surrender totally to Jesus Christ (if you're not yet a baptized believer).
d. If you are saved but living lukewarm, pray and ask the Lord to give you the desire and boldness to serve Him wholeheartedly.

Reflection Song of the Day: I Give Myself Away by William McDowell.

Journal With God

DAY 5
Believing God's Word

But you must continue to believe this truth and stand firmly in it. Don't drift away from the assurance you received when you heard the good news. ***Colossians 1:23a***

The Bible tells us that God's word is a lamp to our feet and we depend on His word to guide us. Many times, we read the Bible, but do we believe it? When we believe something, then we act accordingly. That means we are doers of the word and not a hearer only (See James 1:23).

We should always be a student of the Word; this will help us to know about God and get to KNOW God. We will also get directions and clarity. We will be equipped for work and know how to overcome sin and the works of the devil.

To draw closer to God requires us to study, meditate and believe God's word.

Prayer

Dear Lord, I don't want to just be a hearer, but I want to be a doer of Your Word. I want to mediate on it day and night so I will never sin against You. I pray that I will continue to hunger and thirst for You as I draw closer to You. In Jesus name. Amen.

Journal Challenge

a. Why should you study the Bible? Why is it important?
b. Is there a difference between reading the Bible and studying the Bible? If so, what is it?
c. How can you be more intentional about your Bible study time?

Don't study to remember; study to understand. It is hard to forget something you have a thorough understanding of.

Reflection Song of the Day: What A Beautiful Name it is by Hillsong.

Journal With God

DAY 6
Personalizing God's Word

And I am certain that God, who began the good work within you, will continue his work until it is finally finished on the day when Christ Jesus returns. **Philippians 1:6**

Reading your Bible is not about getting to know the content of the word; it is about getting to know the Author of the word - personally. We should develop the habit of applying the Word of God personally as if God is speaking His Word directly to and through us.

God's word will change and transform your life when you personalize it.

How do you personalize it? Simply replace your name in place of pronouns and nouns in Scripture.

For example: *Psalms 37:4 – "If I, Crystal, delight myself in the Lord, He will give me, Crystal, the desires of my heart."*

Psalm 23:1-2 – "The Lord is Crystal's shepherd; Crystal shall lack nothing. He makes Crystal to lie down in green pastures. He leads Crystal beside the still waters. He restores Crystal's soul."

Some other Scriptures to reflect on:

"But you belong to God, my dear children. You have already won a victory over those people, because the Spirit who lives in you is greater than the spirit who lives in the world." (1 John 4:4).

"For I can do everything through Christ, who gives me strength." (Philippians 4:13).

Journal Challenge

a. Write five Scriptures that you will spend time to meditate on and personalize over the next seven days.
b. Have you ever thought of the Bible as a love letter to you? Why or why not?
c. Have you ever read your Bible like something to check off on your to-do-list? How can you improve that?

Reflection Song of the day: True Intimacy by David Ruis & Eoghan Heaslip.

DAY 7
True Confessions

But if we confess our sins to him, he is faithful and just to forgive us our sins and to cleanse us from all wickedness.
1 John 1:9

To draw closer to God, we must make a daily habit of confessing our sins to Him. Sin is a barrier so we cannot become comfortable living in sin. Many have used God's love to justify their lifestyle and make excuses that God made them that way.

When we confess, we must be repentant (turn away from sin to righteousness). Yes, God loves us but our sin breaks His heart. We cannot be comfortable knowing that we are breaking our Father's heart. Call on Jesus, confess your sins and move forward in Christ through His Forgiveness.

Lord, help me to turn from my sinful ways. Break me free from anything that breaks Your heart.

Search me, Lord, and make me new. I want my live to reflect You. Amen.

Journal Challenge

a. Today, spend time with Christ confessing your sins to Him. Ask God for His help in your weakness. Journal about this experience.
b. Reflect on how your sinful life have disconnected you from Christ.

Reflection Song of the day: Wide As The Sky by Isabel Davis.

DAY 8
Brand New Free

So if the Son sets you free, you are truly free. **John 8:36**

It is so easy to get comfortable living in sin. It is easy to go back to the world and even easier to use the term, "I am human" as an excuse to remain in a sinful lifestyle. Sin easily takes dominion over us because satan never entices us with foolish things but comes with the most desirous thing in our heart. If we allow this desire for worldly things (sex, fame, money) to be more than our desire to have a true relationship with God, then we easily create idols and get comfortable walking in disobedience/sin.

Not only that but when we go back to that lifestyle, satan comes and condemns us so we feel guilty and worthless because we have disappointed God and sometimes it gets so bad, we believe we can never go back to having a relationship with Him because we have failed so many times and what we have done is too bad so God won't forgive us.

I want to remind you today that the Word of God says once Jesus sets us free, we are free indeed!

So, even if you have slipped or fell down, don't stay down. Get up and walk into your freedom. I once heard in a movie, "sin is like a jail cell, except it's nice and comfy and there doesn't seem to be any need to leave. But the cell door is wide open so you can leave anytime. Until one day it slams shut and there is no way out."

Sometimes the devil allows people to live a life free of trouble because he doesn't want them to turn to God. As long as you have not accepted Jesus Christ as your Savior, you are a slave to satan. But choose today to walk into your true freedom.

Prayer

Dear Lord, help me to walk in your freedom every day. Help me to remember that whatever satan comes with is a LIE from the pit of hell and you have already given me a Brand New Free; true freedom in Christ. Amen.

Journal Challenge

a. Write about the day you decided to be free (the day you gave your life to Christ). What made you do it?
b. If you are not a Christian or you are a backslider, write what is holding you captive from walking in true freedom.

God wants me to remind you that He has already set you free, so it is time to walk through that jail cell before it is too late. Now, it is time to pray and give thanks that Jesus Christ came and set you free.

c. If you are a Christian, write a letter to God thanking Him for the freedom He has given you to have a relationship with Him.

Reflection Song of the day: How Can It Be by Lauren Daigle.

Journal With God

Day 9
Walk In Victory

For I can do everything through Christ, who gives me strength. **Philippians 4:13**

As humans, we are most comfortable with what we are familiar with. We often hold on to what we need to let go of. It could be a relationship that is not right for you or maybe anger or unforgiveness or fear holding you back. For us to walk in victory, we must let go and never look back!

I have had situations that I just refused to move on from, no matter how toxic it was. I believed for years it would get better, but it never did. I had to choose that I would not be stuck in the same place another year and it was time to move forward in Christ. When God delivers you, never look back. If you do, it will be hard to see what is ahead of you and you will find yourself falling back to the same place of bitterness, sadness, resentment, and anger.

To walk in victory, we must stay focused on Jesus. Keep looking towards Him. Let Him be the center of your life.

Allow Him to fight your battles because with Him it is a sure victory.

Victory Prayer

Father, today I choose to let go. I will not hold on to the things that are hurting me. Lord, deliver me from anything that will push me away from You. Cleanse my heart and make me new. Jesus, help me to walk in full victory with You. Amen.

Journal Challenge

a. What do you keep looking back at? Who do you refuse to let go of that may be hindering your growth in Christ?
b. What are you uncomfortable with, but you feel stuck in?
c. Talk to God about letting go and not looking back. Ask God for His help to walk in victory.

Reflection Songs of day: I Can't Go Back by William McDowell and The Anthem (You have won the victory).

Journal With God

Day 10
Filling The Void

O God, you are my God; I earnestly search for you. My soul thirsts for you; my whole body longs for you in this parched and weary land where there is no water. ***Psalm 63:1***

At some point in our lives, we all feel a sense of emptiness. It is that deep feeling that something is missing. So, what do we do? We seek money, sex, career; we take drugs and start drinking or we go partying, clubbing or seek relationships. But guess what, the void is still there.

There is a void in our hearts that ONLY God can fill.

Before we come to Christ, we try to fill our void with education, career, friends, partying and sex, but the feeling never goes away; something ALWAYS felt missing. But when you start to seek Jesus, you will truly start to feel complete!

When Jesus met the lady at the well, He told her that if she drank His living water, she would never thirst again. Many of us are Christians but we still feel empty because we are not living in our purpose.

We are busy doing ministry work, trying to blame the husbands for not doing enough, caught up with parenting and adding more career responsibilities; these are not bad things, but they will not fill the emptiness. We must seek Jesus to fill the void and make us complete.

Prayer

Lord, I pray that You will always remain first in my life. Whenever I am down and alone, remind me to turn to You and not to man or anything else. Give me the strength when I am weak, and I pray that You will fill me up and complete me daily. Amen.

Journal Challenge

a. Reflect on what is taking the place of Jesus in your life. Talk to God about it and tell Him why.
b. Write down the disappointments you have had after trying to fill the void with anything but Jesus.

Reflection Song of the day: There Is A Peace In My Soul by Jermaine Edwards.

Journal With God

Day 11
The Envy Trap

Thieves are jealous of each other's loot, but the godly are well rooted and bear their own fruit. **Proverbs 12:12**

Do you ever find yourself envious of other people? It is only natural; everyone does. It is a part of being human. However, we don't have to act on our feelings. Envy distracts us from what God wants to do in our lives and we must daily try to keep our focus on what God is doing in order to combat the emotion of jealousy that tries to plague us.

To combat envy:

1. We must stop comparing ourselves to others. God has blessed us with all we need to serve Him, so let us focus on that.
2. We must be grateful for what we have. There is someone who desires to have what you have.
3. Let us start celebrating when others achieve good things. We must trust that God has not forgotten about us.

Envy denies God's blessings in our lives. It is an insult to God, and it leads to other sins. Envy is resenting God's goodness to others and ignoring God's goodness to us.

Life on earth is unfair because of sin, not because of God. Our focus should always be on Daddy (Our Heavenly Father).

Prayer

Heavenly Father, forgive me when I compare myself with others. Help me, Jesus, to be satisfied with what You have blessed me with and help me to trust that You have even better and bigger in store for me. Amen.

Other mediation Scriptures: Proverbs 14:30, Romans 12:21, Exodus 20:17, Romans 9:20.

Journal Challenge

a. Write down the areas in your life where you often compare yourself to others? Don't lie! We all have a time when we want something that someone else has.

Now, pray that you will be satisfied with your portion and be grateful for what you have.

Reflection Song of the day: Open The Eyes Of My Heart.

DAY 12
Learning To Be Still

Be still, and know that I am God; I will be exalted among the nations, I will be exalted in the earth. ***Psalm 46:10 – NIV***

Many of us don't know how to be still. Being still means to cease, and this requires quietness in God's presence. In the stillness, the peace of God will be your comfort, give you confidence and encourage you to press on no matter what obstacle you may face.

Make it a priority to spend time in devotion with God and have a meaningful quiet time.

Three ways to practice being still:

1. Schedule and find a quiet place (somewhere you won't be interrupted or distracted).
2. Quiet your mind and relax your body.
3. Reflect on the present - don't be thinking about the past or future.

Christianity is not a legalistic religion; it is a love relationship that requires us to spend time with God daily. Focus your mind on Him. Calm down, relax, and recognize His presence.

Journal Challenge

a. What are some of the distractions you face that prevents you from your daily quiet time?
b. What is the one thing in your daily routine that you don't think you can let go of?
c. Write a prayer to God regarding the challenges you face that prevents you from your quiet time?

Reflection Songs of the day: Fill Me Up and Overflow by Tasha Cobbs.

Day 13
Praying For Your Enemy

But when you are praying, first forgive anyone you are holding a grudge against, so that your Father in heaven will forgive your sins, too. **Mark 11:25**

Years ago, at my church's Singles meeting, the guest speaker told us that one way to forgive our enemies is to pray for them to prosper. It sounded ODD! It is hard enough to forgive them but to pray for blessings and favor to come their way; this would take strength we don't naturally possess.

Many of us will see this topic and say, "But I don't have enemies, so I don't need this challenge." We have all been hurt by someone, treated hostile by someone or there are just people who simply hate on you by your mere existence. So, today, those are the people we keep in mind as we mediate on this devotion. That person who you are fighting to forgive; even that person who you know is fighting to forgive you.

So, that weekend I tried it; I spent three days really praying and crying out to God for some people who had done me wrong and shockingly it worked. I had forgiven them but when I started to pray for their prosperity, my heart began to soften and the anger, resentment and hurt began to turn into love. It is amazing when you pray for someone often how you realize you cannot stay mad at them.

The Bible tells us to love our enemies and pray for those who persecute us. If we truly want a heart like Jesus and get all the blessings He has in store for us, we must obey His commands. God repeatedly tells us to love our enemies, forgive them and pray for them.

When you find it hard to forgive, think about how much you have done. We don't deserve God's forgiveness but yet He freely gives us when we run to Him. Forgiveness doesn't mean you are weak or what they did was right; it simply releases them into the hands of God so He can deal with them.

Other mediation Scriptures: Proverbs 25:21, Matthew 18:21-22, Ephesians 4:32.

Let us Pray

Dear Lord, help me to forgive those who have hurt me, persecuted me, abandoned me, betrayed me, and prayed against me. Lord, give me a heart like Yours daily. Give me the strength to pray for my enemies. Amen.

Journal Challenge

a. Today, make a list of all those who have harmed, disappointed, hurt or betrayed you. This could include your parents who abandoned you, your best friend who betrayed you, former teachers who spoke negative words over your life, your husband or boyfriend who broke your heart, even your church mates or coworkers who gossiped about you.
b. START PRAYING for them. Pray that God will help you to forgive them but also pray that God will bless and favor them. Write about this experience in your journal. When you just start praying for them, it won't be easy, it might not even be sincere at first, but I promise you that as you continue daily, it will get easier and you will feel at peace.

Reflection Song of the day: You Are My Strength by Maranda Curtis.

Day 14
Understanding Your Purpose

I knew you before I formed you in your mother's womb. Before you were born I set you apart and appointed you as my prophet to the nations. **Jeremiah 1:5**

Each one of us has a purpose in life; the problem is that many of us don't realize or acknowledge that we do. We are busy trying to acquire all the worldly accolades to make us feel fulfilled, then years after we realize how lonely the top really is and how empty we still feel, even after achieving all the material things.

I went on my "purpose" search in November 2013 because I felt there must be more to life than just doing what I wanted to do and achieving all the things I thought I needed to. There is no way life is just about working, going to school, partying, looking cute and getting married; but for us to know our true purpose, we MUST seek the Creator. It is amazing the woman God is molding me into; the things He has revealed, the visions He placed in my heart. I have to ask, "Lord, can I do all of this?" I am then reminded that, *"For I can do everything through Christ, who gives me strength." (Philippians 4:13).*

If you are not sure what your purpose is; here are a few that we all have in common:

1. We exist to worship the one true and living God.
2. We are called to fellowship with each other.
3. We must serve each other (be our brother's/sister's keeper).
4. We must share the gospel of Jesus Christ.

In doing these things, we all still have a specific part to play in this world. We all have something to do, but you must seek God to find out exactly why you were placed on this earth. You must pray earnestly for it to be revealed and you must use your gifts and talents for God's glory.

Remember, it doesn't matter if your parents said they did not plan for you or you were a mistake or if your parents abandoned you or if you were adopted. God thought about you before you were placed in your mother's womb and there is purpose for your existence.

Other mediation Scriptures: Proverbs 19:21, 1 Peter 2:9.

Purpose Prayer

Lord, help me to live a life with a sense of purpose and to understand the calling You have on my life. Create in me a clean heart, Abba Father, that understands You did not make me by mistake. You took time and effort to create my innermost being. I am special because I was made by You. Thank You that You will work all things for my good. In Jesus' name. Amen.

Journal Challenge

a. What do you think is your purpose? What did God create you for? Write your answers in your journal. If you don't know, start to pray and ask God to reveal it to you because life without purpose is just existing.
b. Today is all about discovering yourself. Write how you can contribute to this life. What contribution do you want to make to impact others?

Reflection Song of the day: You Know My Name by Tasha Cobbs.

Journal With God

Day 15
Don't Be In A Hurry

Do not be in a hurry to leave the King's presence. ***Ecclesiastes 8:3a - NIV***

Having a quiet time is important in our Christian life and spiritual growth. People's quiet time may differ in terms of format but, overall, it is simply spending time with God to meditate, listen, read His word and praise, etc.

God desires alone time with us. He wants a personal relationship with us. God knows the intimate details of our lives, such as the number of hairs on our heads (See Luke 12:7). He invites us to come to Him and know Him. When we desire to know God intimately, we will seek Him and humble ourselves before Him. There are some days you may not feel like spending time with Him but you must do it anyway. The more time you spend with Him, the more you will want to spend time with Him. And do not be in a hurry to leave God's presence.

We will never be able to achieve closeness with God until we invest time and effort in making quiet time a priority.

1 Peter 2:1-2 urges us to yearn for the word of God. As we study the word and it transforms us, our spirit, mind, and body will become one with God. That is what true intimacy is about.

Journal Challenge

a. Have you ever thought about your quiet time as an intimate conversation with God? Why or why not?
b. Describe your quiet time routine; how can it be improved?
c. What do you need to change about your schedule so you can be more consistent with your quiet time with God?

Reflection Song of the day: Your Presence is Heaven to Me by Israel Houghton.

Journal With God

Day 16
Draw Closer Through Prayer

I tell you, you can pray for anything, and if you believe that you've received it, it will be yours. ***Mark 11:24***

Many of us pray as a last resort, instead of making it our first priority. Prayer should never be something we are forced to do. It is a time to communicate with our loving Father. When we begin to develop a prayerful relationship with God, we will hear God's voice with greater clarity.

I learnt this acronym when going to God in prayer: A.C.T.S - **A**cknowledge Him, **C**onfess our sins, **T**hank Him for all He has done and **S**hare your requests/desires.

When we go before God, practice this model, and watch your prayer life change. Remember, pray with faith; worry about nothing; pray about everything.

Prayer is talking to God and it is very powerful. When you pray, pour out your soul. Be natural and honest with God. Tell Him how you feel. Pray out LOUD. It keeps your mind on track and enables you to stay focused.

It is in sincerity of prayer that true intimacy in our relationship with God takes place.

Journal Challenge

a. What is your biggest struggle with prayer? Is it finding time? Is it focus?
b. Think of two practical ways you can increase or improve your conversation with God and put them into practice today.
c. Write down a prayer list (everything you want to pray for; it can be about you or anyone else).

Reflection Song of the day: House of Prayer by Eddie James.

Journal With God

Day 17
Draw Closer To God Through Praise

I will praise the Lord at all times. I will constantly speak his praises. **Psalm 34:1**

Praise to God is acknowledging, honoring and blessing God for who He is and for what He has done. Praise brings pleasure to God and we were created to praise Him. Our praise brings an awareness of God's presence by creating an atmosphere that moves us into the presence of God.

Our praise is also a weapon and we should always praise God.

Praise shifts our focus off ourselves and our problems and on to God and His worthiness. Our spirit is refreshed when we praise God, and it paves the way for His power to be displayed. Our praise draws us closer to God.

Prayer (copied from Tony Evans)

Mighty God, I come before You with thanksgiving and I extol You with praise. You are the King, the great God; the great King above all. I enter Your courts with thanksgiving and into Your presence with a heart of gratitude as well. Thank You that You have chosen me as Your heir to Your kingdom, that I am a child of the King and by virtue of my relationship with You, through your son, Jesus Christ, I am entitled to all the spiritual blessings that You have for me in Your kingdom. Thank You for Your abundant favor. In Jesus name. Amen.

Journal Challenge

a. What are some of the hindrances to praising God? How can we eliminate them?
b. Why should we praise God and what happens to us when we do?
c. Reflect on your favorite praise song and write your experience when you listen to it.

Reflection Song of the day: More Than Anything by Lamar Campbell.

Journal With God

Day 18
Draw Closer to God through Journaling

Then the Lord said to me, "Write my answer plainly on tablets, so that a runner can carry the correct message to others." ***Habakkuk 2:2***

Journaling is simply a way of recording your journey with God. It helps us to pay more attention to God and it is a way to see how God is working in our lives.

Journaling is a therapeutic method that helps you release the pain of hurtful memories. Journaling also inspires your faith. When we record our answered prayers, our faith grows.

Journaling helps us to set spiritual goals that allows us to track our progress and helps with our growth. David wrote his thoughts, experiences, and revelations and that is how we can now read the Psalms. Through journaling, we can track our own revelations, face our fears, and cultivate a deeper spiritual connection.

Listening to the Holy Spirit and journaling what He says will transform your life. It will give you peace, wisdom, hope, healing, direction, stability and build your confidence.

Journal Challenge

a. List five benefits of how journaling draws you closer to God.
b. How does journaling help with listening to God?

Reflection Song of the day: King of My Heart by Steffany Gretzinger & Jeremy Riddle.

Journal With God

Day 19
Endure Hard Times

For our present troubles are small and won't last very long. Yet they produce for us a glory that vastly outweighs them and will last forever. **2 Corinthians 4:17**

Sometimes life gets HARD! There are times in our lives we wonder, "Why me?" "I don't think I can handle this anymore." "It's just too much."

During this time, it is so easy for us to forget God. When we are facing the trial, grief or struggle, we easily forget what God has done for us or what He is doing behind the scenes.

We need to daily pull from the source of hope, faith, love and strength: Jesus Christ. It is not easy to watch your relationship/marriage die after investing so much years. It is hard when health is deteriorating and you wonder if you are being punished. It is hard to lose a love one (parent, child, friends). It is hard when the bills are piling up, but you don't see a source of income to pay them; but we must find that place where we know God's grace and mercy will take us through during those hard times.

If Jesus had to suffer, then we certainly will not be exempted, but the Word of God says that trouble won't last forever and joy comes in the morning.

We need to trust God even more during the hard times. He is in control. He did not promise a perfect life, but He promised that He will be there with us in every circumstance.

So, mourn if you must, cry if you must, scream if you must but PRAY and have FAITH that you will rise again.

Endurance Prayer

> Heavenly Father, help me to remember that no matter how dark my situation may become, You are the light of my life. Thank You for Your grace and mercy that takes me through every hard time in my life. Lord, the enemy tried to destroy me but because of You, I am still standing and for that I am so grateful. Thank You, Lord, that Your hands are on my life and there is nothing too hard for me to handle because I know You will take me through. In Jesus' name. Amen.

Other mediation Scriptures: Psalm 118:8, 1 Peter 4:12-13, Psalm 27:14, Matthew 5:3-4.

Journal Challenge

a. Today, take the time to write down everything you have been though. Think about it; what good came out of that bad situation?
b. What lesson(s) did you learn or are you learning during your hard times?

Remember, whatever you are going through, or have been through, is permitted to strengthen you; it may not seem that way now, but I encourage you to pray and trust God like never before.

Reflection Song of the day: Made A Way by Travis Greene.

Journal With God

Day 20
Draw Closer to God Through Thanksgiving

Always be joyful. Never stop praying. Be thankful in all circumstances, for this is God's will for you who belong to Christ Jesus. ***1 Thessalonians 5:16-18***

Sometimes life can get so overwhelming and it seems like there is nothing to be thankful about. The bills are piling up, job is stressing, relationship is a wreck, health deteriorating, school feels overwhelming, finances are lacking, and things just doesn't seem to be getting better no matter how hard we pray.

We all have those moments! But the Word of God says we should be thankful in all things. Victory comes when we start to find things during the tough times to be thankful for. The fact you are alive reading this devotion is more than enough reason to be thankful. Today is a new day for things to get better and even if it doesn't, be thankful and trust God; He will work it out.

Rejoice always in good times and bad times. Give thanks because as much as you believe your situation is bad, there is someone going through worse. Give thanks because God has not forgotten about you, even if your emotions tell you otherwise. I guarantee He has not; so give thanks.

Prayer

Abba Father, in everything I give You thanks. It doesn't matter how I feel and what I am going through, I am thankful today for who You are and all You have blessed me with. I pray even in hard times that I will always remember to give You thanks. In Jesus' name. Amen.

Journal Challenge

a. Write twenty things in your life that you are thankful for. If you cannot find twenty, write as much as you can and start rejoicing for them.
b. Why do you think thanksgiving is so important to drawing closer to God?

Reflection Song of the day: Thank You for being God by Travis Greene.

Day 21
Conquering Temptation

God blesses those who patiently endure testing and temptation. Afterward they will receive the crown of life that God has promised to those who love him. ***James 1:12***

We are all prone to fall into temptation. It is a constant struggle to stay on the path God has for us because the enemy knows that God has great plans for our lives, and he thinks we are dumb enough to fall for a few moments of pleasure.

Anything we desire can tempt us. James 1:14 says we are drawn away by our desires, so money can tempt us, power tempts us and sexual desire is the most popular temptation. Personally, this was my biggest struggle. I struggled just to stay on the path that God paved for me.

Anyone can fall into temptation but 1 Corinthians 10:13 says God will always give us an escape route. We must remember that we have been given the power to conquer the temptation, but we must follow the Word of God and flee from the lust that cause us to be weak and not try to see how far we can go before we surrender.

You may wonder how conquering temptation fits into drawing closer to God. Unrepentant sins hinder our blessings. God is holy and He has called us to be holy also, but if we keep falling for the same temptation, then we are pushing ourselves further and further from Him.

We must resist the devil and he will flee from us. Conquer your temptation with the Word of God and lots of prayer.

Temptation Prayer

Lord, help me to be strong in mind and spirit so I don't fall into any traps of the enemy. In the name of Jesus, I break every stronghold that temptation has on me. Lord, be my Source, my Light and my Guide. Help me, Lord, to flee and keep me strong from anything that tempts me. Amen.

Journal Challenge

a. Today, we begin to conquer and gain victory over the enemy. Write a letter to God about your temptations and repent if you have been falling. Repenting brings you closer to Christ and further from the enemy.

b. Find and write down Bible verses that ministers to you about resisting temptation. Most of all, pray for the strength to flee from temptation when it presents itself.

Reflection Song of the day: More Than A Conqueror by Rondell Positive.

Journal With God

Day 22
Hearing God's Voice

> *My sheep listen to my voice; I know them, and they follow me. I give them eternal life, and they will never perish. No one can snatch them away from me.* **John 10:27-28**

If you hear God's voice now, would you recognize it?

Listening to God's voice is like listening to anyone; we must be intentional. We cannot hear God if our minds are distracted. We hear God's voice through His Word (Scriptures), through Prayer, a prophetic word, when Holy spirit speaks to our heart and confirmation of a word, etc.

The Word of God says that the sheep knows the voice of the shepherd. That means we must first have a relationship with Jesus Christ before we can truly hear God's voice.

Many people are seeking to hear God through some dramatic voice or thunder from heaven but, like Elijah, in the peace (stillness), God will speak.

Prayer

Teach me to listen, Holy Spirit, to Your voice; in busyness and in boredom, in certainty and doubt, in noise and in silence. Amen.

Journal Challenge

a. Have you ever heard the voice of God speaking directly to you? What was the experience like?
b. How can you prepare your heart to hear from God daily?
c. How will you know it is God's voice you hear and not another voice?

Reflection Song of the day: More Of You by Kevin Downswell.

Journal With God

Day 23
Broken For His Glory

And we know that God causes everything to work together for the good of those who love God and are called according to his purpose for them. **Romans 8:28**

We all have a different story; we all face different fears, insecurities and, sometimes, total brokenness. We go through times where the pain is so devastating that we question God and start to doubt that He has plans to prosper us (See Jeremiah 29:11). But, today, I want to tell you that God will not allow the pain that you have experienced throughout your life to be wasted.

We are broken for God's glory!

God wants to use our trials, struggles, brokenness and weakness to show His strength. He can turn every single negative situation into good and work miracles in our lives.

In brokenness, God is most glorified!

Remember, Moses stuttered, David committed adultery, Paul had a thorn in his flesh. It is in hard times we need to be desperately dependent on God because our own strength is nothing.

Through my time of brokenness; when I was pregnant in church, I felt like I had no one or nothing and that was when I really got close to God and He gave me strength that I did not even thought I possessed. Years later, I can share my testimony to help and remind someone that God is a merciful God and He will take us through our rough times, if we allow Him.

You need to remember that trials, pain or mess can either build you or break you but if we TRUST God during those times, He will not just build us but He will strengthen us enough to help someone else who is going through something similar. There is purpose behind your pain.

Prayer

Lord, thank You for the broken periods in my life. It is in those times that I realized I serve a great, big, wonderful God who cares about me. Lord, use my pain to bring You glory in every way. In Jesus' name. Amen.

Journal Challenge

a. Write about your broken period? How did you feel (or how are you feeling)? What was your motivation to not give up (what is helping you to hold on)? Share it with God. Give Him thanks that the victory is already won.

Reflection Song of the day: Gracefully Broken by Tasha Cobbs.

Journal With God

Day 24
Trusting God

Trust in the Lord with all your heart; do not depend on your own understanding. Seek his will in all you do, and he will show you which path to take. **Proverbs 3:5-6**

It is hard to trust someone we don't know. No one meets someone today and tomorrow they just reveal all their life's story to them and start believing everything that person promises. It is similar with God.

Sometimes we really want to trust God about a situation but honestly it is hard because a part of us will doubt if He will come through for us because we really don't know Him as we ought to.

I have had this struggle; wondering if I would get that new job, complete my degree or find a husband. The closer I got to God; it became easier for me to trust that His timing is perfect.

It wasn't always easy though. I made a lot of mistakes doing it my way and falling flat on my face to realize that my desires or plans were not necessarily God's will for my life. I came to the point where I accepted that I can't trust myself or others because we all have limited wisdom, we are sinful, unreliable and easily swayed by emotions. But I must trust the all-wise, all-knowing, all-powerful and loving God who has the best intentions and plans for my life.

You may be facing a dead-end right now; financial, emotional, relational, but God can see a path that you don't know about. If you trust God and keep on moving in faith, even when you don't see a way, He will make a way.

God is showing me daily that the more we trust Him to make decisions for us, the more we trust Him to come through for us, the more peace we will have and the more prosperous our lives will be. We must be patient. God knows what He is doing. God knows what is best for us. He can see the end result; we can't.

Prayer

Dear Lord, help me to trust You fully with all my heart. I want to live the life that You have prepared for me. Father, help me to appreciate Your timing and not to rely on my own. Amen.

a. What do you think God is trying to teach you while you have been delayed?
b. Write in your journal what you are trusting God for now. Take a few minutes to ask Him if it is His will for you.
c. Write a prayer to God asking Him to reveal His desires for your life.

Whatever you are trusting God for today, put it to Him in prayer. If you need a new job, trust Him; if you need a house, trust Him; if you need healing, a financial breakthrough, a new car: trust Him. If you need a husband; trust Him.

Trust God because He can do exceedingly, abundantly, above anything we could ever ask Him for.

Reflection Song of the day: Trust In You by Lauren Daigle.

Day 25
Come To God In Expectancy

O God, you are my God; I earnestly search for you. My soul thirsts for you; my whole body longs for you in this parched and weary land where there is no water. ***Psalm 63:1***

When you come into the presence of God, you should come with anticipation and eagerness. Expect to have a good time fellowshipping with Him and receive a blessing from your time together.

Be prepared to hear from God, experience God, and call on Him. Come to Him with a spirit of expectancy; expecting God to do something in your life; something only He can do.

There is no limit on what we can expect God to do! He is God and He is bigger than any of us and He has the power and authority to do those things we ask, seek, desire, and yearn for. What we receive from God depends on our level of expectancy. If we expect little, we will receive little. If we expect mountains to be moved and for Him to do the impossible, then He will.

We must also ensure we have the right attitude when we come to God. In God's eyes, why we do something is far more important than what we do. According to 1 Samuel 16:7, God looks at the heart.

Journal Challenge

a. Why do you desire to draw closer to God? It sounds like a silly question, but motives are important in everything we do.
b. How can you always be in expectancy when you have quiet time?
c. Today, talk with God. Spend quality time in His presence. After you talk, listen so you can hear from GOD. Write about this experience in your Journal.

Reflection Song of the day: We Wait For You (Shekinah Glory).

Journal With God

Day 26
Draw Closer To God Through Worship

For God is Spirit, so those who worship him must worship in spirit and in truth. **John 4:24**

Too often we believe that just singing slow songs means we are worshipping God but that is not the case. Worship is more than just singing. Worship is a lifestyle of reverence and submission to the true and living God. It starts with having the right heart-posture where your motive is to offer reverence, thanksgiving, and total sacrifice to God.

In the Old Testament days, people would come to one place (the temple) to offer worship to God. But when Jesus Christ came, died, and rose again, He gave us access to worship God every day, anywhere, anytime and all the days of our lives.

We are now able to worship God through giving, dancing, clapping hands, bowing down, treating others kindly and through singing. God is calling us to draw closer to Him through a lifestyle of worship; this means at every moment we can adore His creation, give thanks for blessings seen or unseen, pray without ceasing, love others as we love ourselves and being obedient to His commands.

While we do express worship through our emotions (crying, laughing), be conscious that worship is more than an emotional high you feel because you like a song. Again, it is all about a heart that is submitted to acknowledging, reverencing, and experiencing God. We need to know who God is through knowing His Word, not just thanking Him for all He has done but for who He is (as the song writer says, "In the good times and bad times, HE is still God and worthy to be worshipped").

Worship is not about you feeling God; it is about God feeling good as you surrender your whole being to Him.

Prayer

Jesus, I worship You. Abba, I worship You. Holy Spirit, I worship You because You are truly worthy to be praised and adored. Daddy, help me to experience deeper intimacy with You through my worship. Lord, I offer my body as a living sacrifice, holy and pleasing to You and I pray that I will daily learn how to worship You as a lifestyle and not just an emotional experience. Father, I thank You that my experience with You after today will elevate my reverence and adoration of You for who You are and not just what You can do. I bless and honor You. I love You, Jesus, with all my being. In Your name I pray. Amen.

Journal Challenge

a. What do you believe worship is?
b. Describe how you will worship God as a lifestyle.
c. How can you offer true worship to God in every experience you have?

Reflection Song of the day: The Heart of Worship by Matt Redman.

Day 27
Draw Closer To God Through Fasting

All that time I had eaten no rich food. No meat or wine crossed my lips, and I used no fragrant lotions until those three weeks had passed. **Daniel 10:3**

Fasting is voluntarily abstaining from food, drink, sleep or sex to focus on a period of spiritual growth. It is when we humbly deny something of the flesh to glorify God, enhance our spirit, and draw closer to God to experience intimacy with Him.

The purpose of fasting is to take our eyes off the things of this world and focus on God. Fasting is a way to demonstrate to God and to ourselves that we are serious about our relationship with Him.

While food-fasting is the most popular and Biblical way, many have realized there are other things that could keep us away from God, such as internet, television, and other leisure activities, so some individuals may choose to fast from these distractions.

There are two things you want to make note of when fasting:

1. Fasting without prayer is just starving. The time you spend in fasting is more beneficial and will invite greater strength if you open and close your fast with a prayer and spend time in sincere prayer during the fast.
2. Fasting for a specific purpose is an exercise in controlling desire. We fast even when it is difficult because we want something else more than we want food. Choose a purpose that will motivate you to rely more heavily on God, to pray often and to strengthen your faith.

During your fast, be specific with what you want God to do for you, so when He comes through, you will know. There is nothing too hard for Him to do.

For you to really draw closer to God, it is highly recommended that you choose a time to fast. It could be one day, three days or twenty-one days; it is up to you and how you believe God is leading you. To grow in intimacy, you must deny your flesh and seek God.

Prayer

Lord, I want to have a greater urge to spend time with You and get to know You more, and I know fasting is a way to do so. Give me a greater desire and help me to fast from food or anything else that may distract me from growing in You. Thank You for the breakthrough that is coming in my life because my eyes are focused on You. Amen.

Journal Challenge

a. When will you be fasting and how long?
b. What is the purpose of your fast? What are you specifically seeking God for during your fast?
c. What Scripture will be your focus during your time with God?

Refection Song of the day: You Deserve It by J.J. Hairston.

Day 28
Draw Closer To God Through Vulnerability

Search me, O God, and know my heart; test me and know my anxious thoughts. Point out anything in me that offends you, and lead me along the path of everlasting life. ***Psalm 139:23-24***

Is it easy to be vulnerable with God? Be honest! Do you find it easy to just be totally naked before God about your pain, desires, dreams, concerns, hurts and fears?

Many people will say yes but let me challenge you to what true vulnerability looks like. When you are vulnerable, you are being "open." Openness can be a little easy because you share some facts about your life. But openness can be just a way to "get attention." Vulnerability goes deeper than openness because it is about exposing. It is not a weakness but it requires you to stop avoiding the REAL issues and come face-to-face about the things you are avoiding.

Sometimes we avoid vulnerability because whoever we share those areas with could possibly hurt us (almost like we give them the handle of the knife to our life).

Vulnerability forces us to experience those hidden feelings. Feelings are what create connection, and feelings are what we fear when we are vulnerable. Feelings like shame, fear, discomfort, indifference, and insecurities must be experienced.

The truth is, God already knows everything about us but getting vulnerable with Him will take your intimacy to a deeper level. Knowing that He has the power to heal every broken area is a beautiful reason why we can be totally real with Him.

Mediate on Psalm 139.

Prayer

(Today, you will write your own prayer to God about needing His help to be vulnerable with Him.)

____

____

____

Journal Challenge

a. What is your darkest secret? Tell it to your Secret-keeper.
b. What is your biggest fear? Tell it to your Strong-tower.
c. How would your life change if you prayed Psalm 139:23-24 every day?

d. Take out a mirror and stare yourself in the eyes for thirty seconds. Write a letter to that person you see and share how you feel about that person you are staring at.

Reflection Song of the day: Reckless Love by Cory Asbury.

Day 29
Draw Closer To God Through Obedience

If you love me, obey my commandments. **John 14:15**

Obedience is God's love language. You cannot say you love God but want to do what you want to do or what the world is telling you to do.

When it comes to obedience, you cannot just think God put laws or rules to stop you from having fun or hinder your progress. It is crucial to see that God is protecting you, loving you and has the best plan for your life.

You obey God, not just out of duty, but out of love and a desire to please Him above everyone else (including yourself).

How do you know what to obey God about? Spend time reading His love letter (the Bible). In the Bible, God shares His will for you and draws you closer to a deeper relationship with Him.

I could share all the reasons why disobedience to God can wreck your life but I don't want you to obey God out of fear (even though fearing God is not a bad thing). This devotional is to empower you to choose to obey God out of a sincere attitude of love and adoration and not fear and condemnation.

Prayer

Daddy, You mean everything to me. Without You, I can do nothing, and I don't want anything else more than to please You. You are my heart's desire, Lord, and I give You my mind, soul, and body. Allow me to let Your love surround me and cast out any fear or doubt I may have about Your love for me. Help me to live in love with You and accept Your will for my life. Lord, I receive Your help to walk out my salvation, to lead a life that brings You joy and brings others joy. Abba, I am thankful that I belong to You. I know You walk by me and hold Your promises true. I bless You. In Jesus name. Amen.

Journal Challenge

a. Sometimes we find it difficult to accept God's love because of our relationship with our earthly father. Maybe he was a good father, and you can trust God more. Maybe he was an absent father, and you don't know if God will leave you too. Maybe he was there but you didn't have the best relationship with him. Whatever your relationship with your earthly father was like, I want you to write a letter to him today expressing how you viewed the relationship.

b. Now that you have dealt with your earthly father, it is time to be intentional about growing into a deeper relationship with your heavenly Father. Schedule a Daddy-child date night this upcoming week and you and God spend some time together.

Reflection Song of the day: So Will I by Hillsong.

Day 30
Double for Your Trouble

Instead of shame and dishonor, you will enjoy a double share of honor. You will possess a double portion of prosperity in your land, and everlasting joy will be yours.
Isaiah 61:7

We are almost at the end of the journal challenge. I encourage you to keep going and growing in Christ.

Zechariah 9:12 says God will restore us double. Isaiah 61:7 says you will receive a double portion.

It is so easy to be focused on the hardships, brokenness, lack, hopelessness, and fears that bombard us in this life. But, today, God promises to restore us with DOUBLE for our trouble. We might be looking for double in quantity, but it might also be double in quality comparing to what we have lost.

When trouble comes from the devil, do not give up and say it is hopeless. WORSHIP GOD. PRAY MORE. TRUST GOD. PRAISE HIM. Speak and declare hope in every situation.

The Bible says there is a season for everything; this means we will have sad times, stressful times, times of lack, etc., but today's promise says when it is the SEASON for happiness, restoration and abundance to come, it will be DOUBLED!

Nothing God does is ever wasted. Even if the situation seems burdensome, choose to find joy and ask the Lord for peace and endurance to get through.

God cannot lie. He honors His Word above His name. He says double, so be confident and declare today that you WILL receive double for your trouble.

Double Portion Prayer

Heavenly Father, my Jehovah Jireh (my Provider), my Jehovah Rapha (my Healer), my awesome God, I come humbly before Your throne giving You thanks for all You have done in my life. Lord, as I walk into my season of joy, help me to let go of sadness, sorrow, doubt, fear, brokenness, sickness, lack, stress, worry and everything that is not of You. Father, I pray for a supernatural release of Your favor and a double portion of Your blessings this season. I stand on Your promise that Your plans are to prosper me and not to harm me. I declare that I am a victor and not a victim. I may have been defeated in the past, but the past has passed, and this is a new day. Lord, prepare me for the next season I am walking into. I receive it, In Jesus' name. Amen.

Journal Challenge

a. What are you afraid to walk into? What is holding you back from experiencing joy? What are you trusting God double for? What situation do you want double restoration in? Double for your trouble challenges your faith to believe for more.
b. Today, talk to God in FAITH that you will walk into a season of happiness. Step out in faith that your double portion awaits you. Share everything with Him about the last thirty days and write about your experience.

Reflection Song of the day: Good Good Father by Chris Tomlin.

Day 31
Put God in First Place

Come close to God, and God will come close to you. Wash your hands, you sinners; purify your hearts, for your loyalty is divided between God and the world. ***James 4:8***

God created us for a relationship with Him. No relationship is built overnight; it takes time to truly get to know each other. The beautiful thing about intimacy with God is that He already knows us (He numbered the hairs on our head), but as James 4:8 says, we must draw close to God.

To draw close to God requires commitment, honesty, sacrifice, trust and faithfulness. That means we must be intentional about pursuing an intimacy and maintaining a relationship with God.

Prayer

Dear Lord, I have experienced You in a new way for the past thirty-one days and I pray that this is the beginning of a consistent devotional life and spending time with You. Lord, help me to stay hungry and thirsty for Your righteousness and help me to wholeheartedly seek Your kingdom first and pursue a deep, personal relationship with You. Thank You for the work You have started in me and I know You will complete it. Amen.

Journal Challenge

a. Is your relationship with God the most important in your life? What is the evidence in your life that this is true?
b. Reflect on the past thirty-one days; is there any improvement in your quiet time with God? If so, journal about the new experience(s). If not, how can you improve?

Reflection Song of the day: First by Lauren Daigle.

Guess what?

You made it through the thirty-one days! You made it through the challenge.

Give yourself a pat on the back, round of applause or a big hug. I know heaven is rejoicing with you. I hope you are proud of yourself also.

Remember, you are as close to God as you choose to be.

"The further away you get from God, the more your life is troubled. The closer you get to God, the more your life is transformed."

~ Rick Warren

Now, that you have started this journey, I beg you not to stop. Deepen your intimacy as you become more like Christ. The meaning of life is "JESUS." Knowing and loving God is our greatest privilege.

"Everything else is worthless when compared with the infinite value of knowing Christ Jesus my Lord. For his sake I have discarded everything else, counting it all as garbage, so that I could gain Christ."

~ (Philippians 3:8).

Thank you!

I appreciate you for joining us on this 31-Day Journal Challenge.

If this challenge was helpful for you, let me hear from you. Send me an email at info@crystaldaye.com or connect with me on Facebook (www.facebook.com/crystalsdaye) or Instagram (www.instagram.com/crystalsdaye) and let me know all about your breakthrough and progress. I can't wait to connect.

I love you and God loves you more,

Crystal

Meet Crystal

I am so excited that you decided to take a leap of faith and invest in deepening your intimacy with God. Let me introduce myself: I am Crystal Daye, best-selling author of the books "Living A Royal Reality" and "Empowered For Such A Time As This," entrepreneur, international speaker and Christian empowerment coach for life and business. As the COO of DayeLight Publishers and Christian Coaches Alliance, I specialize in inspiring and equipping kingdom women and aspiring leaders to confidently clarify their calling and increase their influence and impact so they can passionately pursue their purpose. I know that God has a great plan for you, and it is my purpose to help you be the best God has called you to be.

I encourage you to visit my website to see how else I can serve you on this journey. As a certified Christian life coach, I understand that God created and equipped you for a specific purpose, which is unique to you. As your coach, I partner with the Holy Spirit to help you fulfill your God-given destiny and define success for you as God sees it rather than how the world sees it. Please feel free to book a complimentary thirty-minute Clarity Breakthrough Session with me to see how I can empower you to live purposefully, fearlessly, and confidently in your divine calling.

For coaching, speaking and workshop training inquiries, please contact Crystal at info@crystaldaye.com or visit our website @ www.crystaldaye.com

www.ingramcontent.com/pod-product-compliance
Lightning Source LLC
LaVergne TN
LVHW010101110826
845155LV00028B/443